PERSPECTIVES ON AMERICAN PROGRESS

ROSA PARKS
STAYS SEATED

DUCHESS HARRIS, JD, PHD
WITH HEATHER C. HUDAK

Core Library

An Imprint of Abdo Publishing
abdopublishing.com

Cover image: Rosa Parks is fingerprinted at the police station after her second arrest for not giving up her bus seat.

abdopublishing.com

Published by Abdo Publishing, a division of ABDO, PO Box 398166, Minneapolis, Minnesota 55439. Copyright © 2019 by Abdo Consulting Group, Inc. International copyrights reserved in all countries. No part of this book may be reproduced in any form without written permission from the publisher. Core Library™ is a trademark and logo of Abdo Publishing.

Printed in the United States of America, North Mankato, Minnesota
032018
092018

THIS BOOK CONTAINS
RECYCLED MATERIALS

Cover Photo: Gene Herrick/AP Images
Interior Photos: Gene Herrick/AP Images, 1; Don Cravens/The LIFE Images Collection/Getty Images, 4–5, 17, 43; AP Images, 8; Russell Lee/Farm Security Administration/Office of War Information Black-and-White Negatives/Library of Congress, 10; Joe Holloway, Jr./AP Images, 12–13; Grey Villet/The LIFE Picture Collection/Getty Images, 15; © 1956 Dr. Martin Luther King, Jr., © renewed 1984 Coretta Scott King/Don Cravens/The LIFE Images Collection/Getty Images, 20–21; Red Line Editorial, 23, 40; Jim Peppler/Alabama Department of Archives and History, 28–29; Harrity/AP Images, 31; Ira Bostic/Shutterstock Images, 34–35

Editor: Marie Pearson
Imprint Designer: Maggie Villaume
Series Design Direction: Ryan Gale

Library of Congress Control Number: 2017962654

Publisher's Cataloging-in-Publication Data

Names: Harris, Duchess, author. | Hudak, Heather C., author.
Title: Rosa Parks stays seated / by Duchess Harris and Heather C. Hudak.
Description: Minneapolis, Minnesota : Abdo Publishing, 2019. | Series: Perspectives on American progress | Includes online resources and index.
Identifiers: ISBN 9781532114946 (lib.bdg.) | ISBN 9781532154775 (ebook)
Subjects: LCSH: Parks, Rosa, 1913-2005--Juvenile literature. | Race discrimination--Juvenile literature. | Civil rights movements--Juvenile literature. | African American women civil rights workers--Biography--Juvenile literature.
Classification: DDC 323.092 [B]--dc23

CONTENTS

SEGREGATION AND OPPRESSION

December 1, 1955, had been a long day for Rosa Parks. She worked as a seamstress, sewing clothes in Montgomery, Alabama. She was tired and eager to get home. Parks boarded the Cleveland Avenue bus. It was more crowded than normal that day. Most of the seats for black people were taken. She found a seat in the row right behind the seats for white people only and sat down.

After a few more stops, there were no more seats left in the white part of the bus. Black people started to make room for

Rosa Parks, *in dark coat*, boarded the bus like she did most other days.

5

white riders. But one white man was left standing. That's when the bus driver, James F. Blake, looked back. He told Parks and three other black people sitting near her to give up their seats. African Americans were expected to stand so that white people could sit. The others rose. They moved to the back of the bus. Most days, Parks agreed to move too. But she'd had enough of giving in to unfair segregation laws. She remained seated. Blake asked Parks if she was planning to stand up. She simply said, "No." He said he would have Parks arrested. She replied, "You may do that." Blake left the bus and came back with two police officers. They hauled Parks off to City Hall. She was fingerprinted, photographed, and charged. Then she was placed in a prison cell.

Parks took a stand by staying seated on that bus. That small act changed the course of her life and the lives of many others forever. She showed people that it wasn't okay to treat black people differently. People across the city—and even the entire country—took notice. Parks quickly became one of the best-known faces of the American civil rights movement.

History of Inequality

The American civil rights movement took place from the mid-1950s to the late 1960s. African Americans did not have the same civil rights and freedoms as white people. In the southern states, oppression and segregation were common since the American Civil War (1861–1865) and the end of slavery. Over time, black people began to take action. They hoped to gain fair and equal treatment for all people. In the 1930s, the National Association for the Advancement of Colored People

NAACP FOR CIVIL RIGHTS

The NAACP is a civil rights group that formed in 1909 in Springfield, Illinois. It tries to make the world a fair and equal place for all people no matter their race. The NAACP holds events to help spread the word about why civil rights matter. Today, the NAACP has more than 500,000 members around the world.

The NAACP used lawyers including Thurgood Marshall to fight segregation in the courts.

(NAACP) began working to remove segregation from society.

Growing Up

Rosa Parks was born Rosa Louise McCauley in Tuskegee, Alabama, on February 4, 1913. When Rosa was two years old, her parents separated. She moved to Pine Level, Alabama, with her mother and younger brother, Sylvester. They lived on a farm with her grandparents, who had formerly been enslaved.

Rosa went to the local African American school. It

RECY TAYLOR

In 1944 a group of white men assaulted Recy Taylor. The police arrested no one though they knew who the men were. So the NAACP sent Parks, one of their investigators. The sheriff threatened Parks as she interviewed Taylor. Parks exposed the case in newspapers. Despite her hard work and public outrage, two juries refused to charge the men.

was a one-room schoolhouse that the black community built themselves. It did not have enough supplies for all of the students. Rosa walked to school every day while white children rode the bus to a nice, new school. Rosa had to leave school in her junior year to care for her sick grandmother. She planned to return to get her high school diploma, but then her mother

Making black people use separate drinking fountains was just one way white people tried to promote segregation.

became ill. Sylvester went to work while Rosa cared for their mother.

Segregation was so severe that Rosa sometimes wondered if the water white people drank from their separate fountains tasted the same as the water she drank. At night, she could hear the Ku Klux Klan (KKK) march through the streets. The KKK did not believe black people should have the same rights and freedoms as white people. Members set fire to black homes and churches. Rosa feared they would one day come for her family. Some nights she slept with her clothes on in case she had to run away quickly.

In 1931 Rosa was working as a housekeeper when a friend introduced her to Raymond Parks. Rosa and Raymond married on December 18 the next year, and Rosa McCauley became Rosa Parks. With Raymond's support, Parks got her high school diploma in 1934. Raymond promoted civil rights. It wasn't long before Parks did too.

EXPLORE ONLINE

Chapter One discusses Parks's childhood. The article at the website below goes into more depth on this topic. Does the article answer any of the questions you had about Parks's life?

ROSA LOUISE PARKS BIOGRAPHY
abdocorelibrary.com/rosa-parks

THROUGH PARKS'S EYES

I n December 1943, Parks became the first woman to join the Montgomery chapter of the NAACP. She served as the group's youth leader. She heard countless stories of unfair treatment and abuse toward African Americans.

Parks began taking regular stands against the oppression. White people often got away with crimes they committed against black people. Parks worked to make sure these criminals were punished. She also worked to change everyday racism. One rainy day in 1943, Parks tried to enter a bus through the front door. At the time, black people had to

Parks was active in the civil rights movement long before her famous bus ride.

pay at the front and then walk to the back door to enter. The bus driver ordered Parks off the bus. She had to walk 5 miles (8 km) in the rain. Parks sometimes drank from the water fountain for white people. She wanted to let people know it was not okay to treat people badly because of the color of their skin. These acts led up to her refusal to stand on the bus on December 1, 1955.

CLAUDETTE COLVIN TAKES A STAND

Parks was not the first to refuse to give up her seat on a bus. On March 2, 1955, 15-year-old Claudette Colvin was told to stand up so a white person could sit down. Colvin refused. She was arrested. Civil rights leaders thought about using Colvin's case to build a legal case against segregation laws. But they decided Colvin's inexperience in the movement and her fiery temperament would not be the best face for the cause. Parks, an experienced, calmer person with a career, became their pick.

Word Gets Out

Word of Parks's arrest for not leaving her bus seat spread quickly through the black

Even in the rain, black commuters walked to work in support of Parks and so their money would not fund the racist bus system.

community. Many people believed Parks wasn't feeling well enough to stand up that day. She later said that she felt just fine. She was simply tired of being mistreated. She knew her life would never change if she never did anything about it.

Parks's trial took place on December 5. At the courthouse, 500 supporters came for the trial. It lasted only half an hour. She was found guilty and ordered to pay $14 in fines and court fees. That same day, approximately 40,000 African Americans refused to take the bus. They carpooled or walked to work instead. Parks had no idea

Parks, *left*, rode a desegregated bus after the boycott.

that refusing to give up her seat that day would inspire a movement to put an end to segregation in the South.

After the Boycott

Parks and her husband lost their jobs. They could not find work in Alabama. They moved to Detroit, Michigan, in 1957. For the first few years, they lived in a small house with Parks's brother. Parks worked out of the basement as a seamstress. They had little money. Parks struggled with feeling lonely. She also felt like she might be losing her mind. White people had treated black people unfairly for a long time. It had been so long even many black people felt her actions were extreme and distanced themselves from her. But despite the challenges, Parks continued to fight for civil rights.

STRAIGHT TO THE
SOURCE

Parks explained the injustices black people faced on buses in Montgomery and how the bus driver's actions drew attention:

In fact some [bus drivers] did tell me not to ride their buses. If I felt that I was too important to go to the back door to get on. And going to the back door after paying your fare in the front would mean sometime that people wouldn't even get on the bus at all because if you couldn't get around fast enough to suit the driver, he would just drive off and leave you standing after you paid your fare. . . . There was nothing different about that day because as I said before, I had from time to time had some confrontation with bus drivers. But the difference that made it, this driver decided to have me arrested and have the policeman to take me to jail. And that did attract more attention than it had if I had just gotten off the bus—on his orders.

Source: "Interview with Rosa Parks." *Eyes on the Prize: Interviews*. Washington University Digital Library, November 14, 1985. Web. Accessed December 13, 2017.

What's the Big Idea?

Take a close look at what Parks said. What drove her to refuse to listen to the bus driver? How did the driver's actions gain more attention than if he had kicked her off the bus?

TAKING ACTION

On the morning of December 2, 1955, Martin Luther King Jr. got a call from Montgomery NAACP president Edgar Nixon. Nixon told King about Parks's arrest. King thought highly of Parks. He and Nixon asked ministers and city leaders to meet that night.

King was tired of inequality and segregation. He was ready to make a change. But he was worried that no one else would support the cause. When he arrived at the meeting that night, his fears were cast aside. More than 40 people turned up for the event. They decided a bus boycott was the best

Parks, *seated*, listened with others as Martin Luther King Jr., *left*, explained the bus boycott plan.

course of action. Black people would quit riding buses, causing the bus system to lose money. King helped write a statement to give to black people. He was so excited that night that he barely slept.

Becoming a Leader

King and his wife Coretta woke early on December 5. They wanted to see if any black people were riding the bus. They watched in awe as one empty bus after another passed by their home. The movement was a success.

Later that afternoon, King met with other black leaders. They formed the Montgomery Improvement Association (MIA). The group would promote the bus boycott. They would also work for better rights for black people in Montgomery. King was elected to head the MIA. He was only 26 at the time. King had been working as a pastor for a little more than a year. He had a wife and baby girl at home. He worried his work with the civil rights movement might put them in harm's way.

LIFE FOR
AFRICAN AMERICANS
IN THE UNITED STATES

This timeline shows what life was like for black people in the mid-1900s. What do you notice about their jobs, pay, and how white people interacted with them? How does this help you understand what civil rights activists were trying to change?

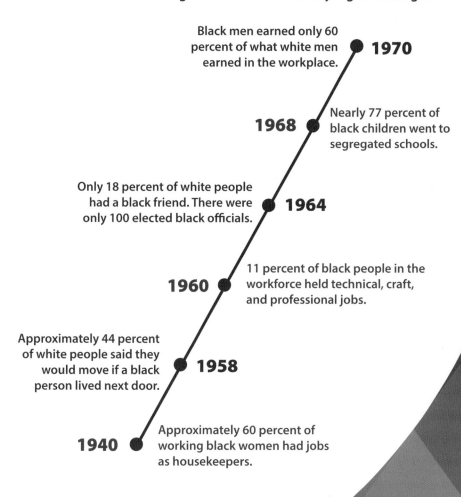

Black men earned only 60 percent of what white men earned in the workplace. **1970**

1968 Nearly 77 percent of black children went to segregated schools.

Only 18 percent of white people had a black friend. There were only 100 elected black officials. **1964**

1960 11 percent of black people in the workforce held technical, craft, and professional jobs.

Approximately 44 percent of white people said they would move if a black person lived next door. **1958**

1940 Approximately 60 percent of working black women had jobs as housekeepers.

WHITE CITIZENS' COUNCIL OPPOSES DESEGREGATION

The White Citizens' Council (WCC) was a group that promoted white supremacy. It was made mainly of white business-class people. There were branches across the South. They had weekly television shows and radio programs. The WCC in Montgomery doubled in size during the bus boycott. Many members terrorized, beat, and killed African Americans and white supporters of the civil rights movement.

He thought white people who were upset about the movement might lash out at them. But he was the perfect choice for the job. As a pastor and a well-educated man, the MIA believed white people would take him more seriously.

That night, King gave his first speech as leader of the MIA. Thousands of African Americans came to hear what he had to say. He spoke about taking a stand for freedom. He urged people to keep the boycott going.

The Boycott Leads to Change

City leaders and the bus company believed the boycott would last only a short time. They thought black people would return to the buses as soon as the next rainfall came. But they did not. Finally city leaders agreed to talk to the MIA. King represented the group.

King explained that black people had been putting up with poor treatment for years. Parks's act simply got people thinking about what they could do to change their own lives. The boycott was the answer. King gave the terms for ending the boycott. King and the MIA were disappointed with the slow response from the city and bus company.

In the meantime, white people became angry with King. He began to get death threats. On January 30, white segregationists bombed King's home. His wife and child were inside. Both were unharmed, but King was shaken by the event.

MOHANDAS GANDHI

Civil rights activists looked to history for protest strategies. Mohandas Gandhi, born in Porbandar, India, in 1869, inspired many. The lawyer practiced Hinduism and believed in living a simple life. Gandhi saw a lot of racism toward Indian people. He led Indians in nonviolent protests against British rule. He was arrested many times. Gandhi was key to helping India gain freedom from Britain in 1947. His nonviolent protests inspired the methods many civil rights activists used.

The next day, the MIA filed a lawsuit demanding segregation to be stopped on city buses. The boycott continued. It lasted 381 days until December 20, 1956, when the US Supreme Court ruled segregation on buses was unconstitutional. The next morning, King rode on the first desegregated bus in Montgomery.

National Civil Rights Leader

King's role in the boycott was just the start of his civil rights work. In 1957 King formed the Southern Christian Leadership Conference. The group took the fight for civil rights across the South. Over the years, King spoke at more than 2,500 civil rights events. He was arrested more than 20 times.

On August 28, 1963, King led the March on Washington. Approximately 200,000 people gathered at the Lincoln Memorial. They wanted justice for everyone. King gave his famous "I Have a Dream" speech. He hoped to achieve equality across America. But on April 4, 1968, a racist named James Earl Ray assassinated King. Yet King's influence lived on.

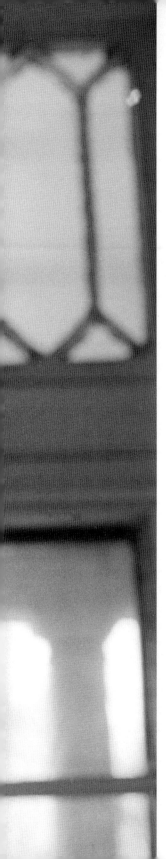

RAYMOND SUPPORTS PARKS

On the night of her arrest, Parks called home to tell her husband and her mother what happened. Raymond was angry that no one had told him sooner. The man who was sitting next to Parks on the bus was their neighbor. He saw the whole thing happen but did not tell Raymond.

That night, Raymond and Parks met with Edgar Nixon and Clifford and Virginia Durr. Clifford was a civil rights lawyer. His wife was an activist. Parks had worked for them. They talked about the arrest. They also talked about

Clifford Durr defended many black people in court even though they often could not pay him for his work.

using Parks's arrest to build a case against segregation laws. Raymond did not like the idea. He thought it would be a very hard case to win.

PERSPECTIVES
FRED GRAY

Fred Gray was a preacher and a lawyer. He defended Parks after she was arrested on the Montgomery bus. He was only the second black lawyer in Montgomery and the twelfth in Alabama at the time. He went on to handle many other key civil rights cases. He worked to help African Americans gain voting rights. He also helped remove segregation in schools. In 1970 he was elected as an Alabama state representative.

Raymond had been a civil rights activist long before he met Parks. He even helped her get involved in the fight for civil rights. But Raymond feared white people would strike back at Parks. He wanted to protect her. Over time, he came around to the idea. Parks called lawyer Fred Gray the next morning to ask him to take her case.

Fred Gray was an influential lawyer for the civil rights movement.

Starting Over

Raymond worked at Maxwell Air Force Base as a barber for many years. He was quite successful. After the bus boycott, he lost his job. He struggled to find work. In 1957 the couple moved to Detroit to start a new life.

Parks traveled often, making appearances for the MIA. Raymond respected his wife and her activism. But it was a challenging time for him. He was left to

ROSA AND RAYMOND PARKS INSTITUTE

In 1987 Parks opened the Rosa and Raymond Parks Institute for Self-Development with her friend Elaine Eason Steele. Parks wanted to honor Raymond's memory. As did Parks, Raymond dedicated his life to helping black people find equality and freedom. The institute helps young people reach their highest potential. It offers programs to help youth gain the skills they need to find good jobs.

answer the many hate calls and death threats at home. Still, he worked hard to maintain their home, make travel plans, and support his wife in everything she did. As did Parks, Raymond firmly believed in equality for black people. He did whatever he could to support the cause. Parks could not have done her work without Raymond's love and support. But after battling cancer for five years, Raymond died on August 19, 1977.

STRAIGHT TO THE
SOURCE

In 2013 President Barack Obama spoke of Parks's contributions at the dedication of a statue of Parks at the US Capitol:

> *Three hundred and eighty-five days after Rosa Parks refused to give up her seat, the boycott ended. Black men and women and children re-boarded the buses of Montgomery, newly desegregated, and sat in whatever seat happened to be open. And with that victory, the entire edifice of segregation, like the ancient walls of Jericho, began to slowly come tumbling down. . . .*
>
> *Rosa Parks tells us there's always something we can do. She tells us that we all have responsibilities, to ourselves and to one another.*

Source: "Remarks by the President at Dedication of Statue Honoring Rosa Parks—US Capitol." *Office of the Press Secretary*. The White House: President Barack Obama, February 27, 2013. Web. Accessed November 29, 2017.

Consider Your Audience

How would you adapt this text for a different audience, such as your parents or friends? Write a blog post for the new audience. How does your post differ from the original, and why?

A MODERN POINT OF VIEW

In February 2012, a black high school student was shot and killed in Florida. Trayvon Martin was just 17 years old. He was unarmed and talking to his girlfriend on the phone at the time. The shooter was neighborhood watch captain George Zimmerman. Zimmerman claimed he shot Martin in self-defense during a struggle. When police learned that Zimmerman had racially profiled Martin, who had committed no crimes, they charged Zimmerman with murder. Then on July 13, 2013, Zimmerman was found not guilty.

Trayvon Martin had been carrying candy and a drink, so protesters brought them to marches.

Alicia Garza, a black activist from Oakland, California, felt like she had been punched in the gut when she heard the verdict. She cried herself to sleep that night. Garza was tired of hearing about attacks on black people. She had a brother and worried something similar could happen to him one day. The segregation of Parks's day was illegal now. But other forms of discrimination remained. Garza felt racism and white supremacy were too common. Garza posted her thoughts on Facebook. She ended her post with the words, "Black people. I love you. I love us. Our lives matter."

Modern-Day Movement

Garza had no idea the impact her words would have. She shared the post with friends, adding the hashtag #blacklivesmatter. Her friends, activists Patrisse Cullors and Opal Tometi, helped spread her message. Soon, the three women were sharing the hashtag all over social media. By January 2015, #blacklivesmatter had inspired a movement.

Garza, Cullors, and Tometi wanted better rights and freedoms for black people, just as Parks had. They wanted to get people thinking about how they could make America a safer place for black people. African Americans are still treated poorly in many parts of the country. But it's not just racists and white supremacists who treat them unfairly. Biases, intentional or not, have led to police officers shooting unarmed black people.

Today, there are more than 40 chapters

CHARLOTTESVILLE RIOTS

In August 2017, hundreds of white supremacists met to protest the removal of a statue in Charlottesville, Virginia. The statue was of a man who supported slavery. Another group of people met to protest the white supremacists. Soon, fights broke out between the two groups. People began to riot. An Ohio man drove a car into the crowd of anti-racism protesters. The man had extreme views about different races. He intended to hurt people. One person was killed and 19 others injured. The event is just one example of the racism that still takes place in parts of the United States today.

of the Black Lives Matter Global Network, which Garza, Cullors, and Tometi founded. Each one holds events and promotes equality for everyone. Their protests mirror the disruption that the bus boycotts caused. Groups gather in public places, disrupting traffic or businesses, hoping to end police brutality.

Parks's Legacy

In 1964 Parks helped get African American lawyer John Conyers elected to Congress. He asked her to join his staff in 1965. Parks worked for Conyers until 1988. She also traveled across the country in support of civil rights events.

Parks received the Presidential Medal of Freedom in 1996. She got the Congressional Gold Medal in 1999. She never stopped helping others stand up for what they believed in. Parks died on October 24, 2005, at 92 years old. Her life was celebrated in a weeklong series of events. Today, she is known as the mother of the modern-day civil rights movement.

Parks's achievements have touched people all around the world. In 2016 the broken-down house where Parks lived after she moved to Detroit was about to be destroyed. American artist Ryan Mendoza wanted to protect it. He believed it should remain as a symbol of everything Parks stood for. He bought the house, took it apart, and shipped it to Germany where he lived. Then, he rebuilt it in his backyard.

The house represents Parks's suffering for civil rights. Mendoza believes the house should be back in the United States. There are few civil rights monuments. Mendoza thinks the

PERSPECTIVES
ALL LIVES MATTER

In response to #blacklivesmatter, some people started using #alllivesmatter. They felt this hashtag expressed that the color of a person's skin shouldn't matter. Today, this hashtag is seen as racist. It takes the focus off of the fact that black people are treated like their lives don't matter. Many people believe it sends the message that white lives should be valued more than black lives.

CIVIL RIGHTS MOVEMENT IN MONTGOMERY

Many historic events took place in Montgomery during the American civil rights movement. This map shows the locations of some of those events and a few important places. Why do you think Montgomery was a place where many people chose to fight for civil rights?

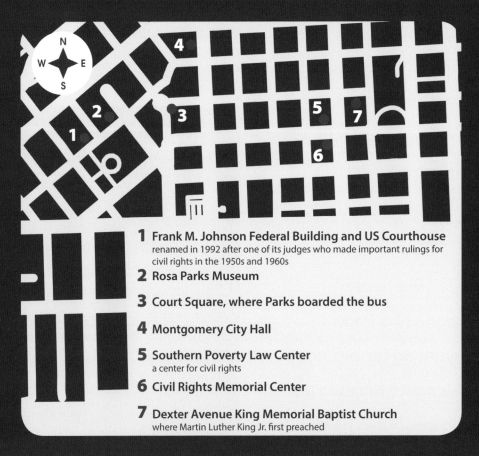

1 **Frank M. Johnson Federal Building and US Courthouse**
renamed in 1992 after one of its judges who made important rulings for civil rights in the 1950s and 1960s

2 **Rosa Parks Museum**

3 **Court Square, where Parks boarded the bus**

4 **Montgomery City Hall**

5 **Southern Poverty Law Center**
a center for civil rights

6 **Civil Rights Memorial Center**

7 **Dexter Avenue King Memorial Baptist Church**
where Martin Luther King Jr. first preached

house would remind people of the importance of her work. He believes it can help people talk about racism today.

In 2017 the Nash Foundation agreed to pay to bring the house back to the United States. But Mendoza was having trouble finding a place to take it. Many well-known museums were full. Mendoza kept on looking. He hoped he could one day find a place worthy of hosting such an important piece of history.

Parks's legacy continues to influence people today. There was no way for Parks to know Americans would see her as a hero decades after her rebellion on segregation. Her story inspires people to this day.

FURTHER EVIDENCE

Chapter Five talks about modern civil rights work. What was one of the main points of this chapter? What evidence does the author provide to support this point? The website at the link below has more information on modern civil rights work. Find a quote that supports the main point of this chapter. Does this quote support the evidence you found in this book? Is it a new piece of evidence?

BLACK LIVES MATTER: WHAT WE BELIEVE
abdocorelibrary.com/rosa-parks

IMPORTANT
DATES

1913
Rosa Louise McCauley is born in Tuskegee, Alabama, on February 4.

1932
McCauley marries Raymond Parks on December 18.

1955
On March 2, Claudette Colvin refuses to give her seat to a white person on a bus. On December 1, Parks refuses to give up her seat on a bus. Police arrest her. On December 2, Martin Luther King Jr. and Edgar Nixon start planning the Montgomery bus boycott. Parks stands trial on December 5.

1956
The Montgomery bus boycott ends on December 20.

1957
Parks and Raymond move to Detroit, Michigan.

1965
Parks begins working for Congressman John Conyers.

1996
Parks receives the Presidential Medal of Freedom.

1999
Parks gets the Congressional Gold Medal.

2005
Parks dies on October 24 at 92 years old.

STOP AND
THINK

Tell the Tale

Chapter One of this book discusses segregation in the South. Imagine you are a living in the 1950s. Write 200 words about how you could take a stand for civil rights.

Surprise Me

Chapter Three discusses Martin Luther King Jr.'s role in the bus boycott. After reading this book, what two or three facts about King did you find most surprising? Write a few sentences about each fact. Why did you find each fact surprising?

Dig Deeper

After reading this book, what questions do you still have about the bus boycott? With an adult's help, find a few reliable sources that can help you answer your questions. Write a paragraph about what you learned.

GLOSSARY

boycott
to refuse to use or do
something as a form
of protest

civil rights
a citizen's rights in daily life

discrimination
unfair treatment of a person
based on race, sex, or
other reasons

movement
a group of people working
together to make a change
in society

oppression
the act of having treated
someone poorly for a
long time

racism
the belief that people
of one race are better
than people of another

segregation
keeping people separated
because of traits such as race

verdict
a judgment or opinion in a
court case

white supremacy
the belief that white people
are better than people of
another race

ONLINE
RESOURCES

To learn more about Rosa Parks and the civil rights movement, visit our free resource websites below.

Visit **abdocorelibrary.com** for free Common Core resources for teachers and students, including vetted activities, multimedia, and booklinks, for deeper subject comprehension.

Visit **abdobooklinks.com** for free additional online weblinks for further learning. These links are routinely monitored and updated to provide the most current information available.

LEARN
MORE

Donohue, Moira Rose. *The Civil Rights Movement through the Eyes of Lyndon B. Johnson*. Minneapolis, MN: Abdo, 2016.

Harris, Duchess. *Civil Rights Sit-Ins*. Minneapolis, MN: Abdo, 2018.

ABOUT THE
AUTHORS

Duchess Harris, JD, PhD

Professor Harris is the chair of the American Studies department at Macalester College and curator of the Duchess Harris Collection of ABDO books. She is the author and coauthor of recently released ABDO books including *Hidden Human Computers: The Black Women of NASA*, *Black Lives Matter*, and *Race and Policing*.

Before working with ABDO, she authored several other books on the topics of race, culture, and American history. She served as an associate editor for *Litigation News*, the American Bar Association Section of Litigation's quarterly flagship publication, and was the first editor in chief of *Law Raza*, an interactive online journal covering race and the law, published at William Mitchell College of Law. She has earned a PhD in American Studies from the University of Minnesota and a JD from William Mitchell College of Law.

Heather C. Hudak

Heather C. Hudak has written hundreds of books for children and edited thousands more. She loves learning about new topics, traveling the world, and spending time with her husband and many pets.

INDEX